# THE OFFICIAL
# WEST HAM
# UNITED
## ANNUAL 2020

Written by **Rob Pritchard**
Designed by **Daniel May**

D0996846

g

A Grange Publication

© 2019. Published by Grange Communications Ltd., Edinburgh, under licence from West Ham Football Club. Printed in the EU.

Photographs © West Ham United Football Club.

ISBN: 978-1-913034-34-4

# CONTENTS

# CLARET ✕ MEMBERSHIP
## 2019/20

**JOIN FOR TICKET PRIORITY AND MORE!**

## CLARET KIDS £25 (UNDER 16)

**Benefits include:**

- ✕ Ticket priority on Premier League and Cup fixtures*
- ✕ £5 discount on all Premier League fixture general sale prices**
- ✕ £10 discount on women's Season Tickets and discounted match tickets
- ✕ Attend PL2 matches at London Stadium for free
- ✕ Additional merchandise discount and offers
- ✕ Exclusive competitions – prize draws for signed shirts, memorabilia and money-can't-buy experiences

- ✕ Two Kids for a Quid Premier League fixtures in the season***
- ✕ Invite to Junior Hammers party for Claret Kids****
- ✕ Under 16 Match ticket price for Category A fixtures in seat bands 4 and 5
- ✕ **Exclusive gift pack** – including branded West Ham backpack, pencil case and stationery set

## IRON BORN £25
### 0-4 YEARS OLD

**If you have a little Hammer in the household, or know someone who has, then this is the Membership for them.**

**IRON BORN** is our starter Membership that lasts until the season our new fan reaches 5 years of age, for a one-off fee of £25.

The Membership includes an exclusive welcome pack with Iron Born lunchbox, plate and cutlery set and drinks beaker, plus the benefits of our Claret Kids Membership.*****

## Become a Claret Member today
### Join now at **eticketing.co.uk/whufc** or call **0333 030 1966**

# WEST HAM UNITED
## THE OFFICIAL ANNUAL 2020

### THIS ANNUAL BELONGS TO:

---

**MY AGE:**

---

**MY SCHOOL:**

---

**MY FOOTBALL TEAM:**

---

**MY POSITION:**

---

**MY FAVOURITE WEST HAM UNITED PLAYER:**

---

**WHERE WEST HAM UNITED WILL FINISH IN THE PREMIER LEAGUE:**

---

WHUFC.COM  f @WESTHAM

 @WESTHAM  @WESTHAM

7

# 8 THINGS YOU (PROBABLY) DIDN'T KNOW ABOUT WEST HAM UNITED!

**1** The Club's first-ever captain was a Scotsman named Bob Stevenson, who skippered Thames Ironworks FC from 1895-97. A versatile player, Barrhead-born Bob could play as a full-back, midfielder or centre forward!

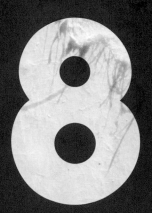

**3** West Ham United's all-time record scorer Vic Watson netted 13 hat-tricks during his 15-year career in Claret and Blue, including six goals in an 8-2 win over Leeds United in February 1929!

**2**  A former West Ham full-back, the Club's first manager Syd King took charge of an amazing 1,038 matches between 1902-32, winning 403 of them.

**4** 1966 FIFA World Cup final hat-trick hero Sir Geoff Hurst scored 68 goals for the Hammers in cup competitions — more than double the 31 managed by second-place Tony Cottee!

**5** West Ham United have played Premier League football at 59 different stadiums, the first of which was the Boleyn Ground in August 1993, while the most-recent new addition was Tottenham Hotspur Stadium in April 2019.

**6** Club captain Mark Noble has been booked a record 95 times in his West Ham career, while his five red cards are the joint-most alongside former skippers Julian Dicks and Steve Lomas!

**7** When West Ham United were promoted from the Second Division in 1980/81, John Lyall's team achieved a record number of 28 home wins from their 42 matches, including an amazing 19 from 21 at home!

**8** Declan Rice became West Ham United's 42nd senior England international when he made his debut against Czech Republic at Wembley in March 2019. The first was George Webb, almost exactly 108 years earlier in March 1911!

# 2018/19 SEASON REVIEW

**The 2018/19 season was one of undoubted progression and development at all levels at West Ham United — on and off the pitch.**

At first-team level, the Board appointed a proven, world-class, Premier League title-winning manager in **Manuel Pellegrini** in June 2018, before investing more funds than ever before in the squad, signing nine senior players and twice breaking the Club's transfer record.

After a slow start to the season, Pellegrini's project has begun to bear fruit in the shape of

entertaining, attacking football in the West Ham tradition, coupled with some outstanding performances and results achieved against some of the biggest clubs in Europe.

At **London Stadium**, with demand to watch the Hammers in action live ever increasing and more than 52,000 Season Ticket holders in place, the capacity was increased to 60,000 shortly after Christmas, enabling West Ham to play in front of the third-highest average home attendance in English football this season, in excess of 58,000.

Following the granting of an **FA Women's Super League** licence in May 2018, the Club appointed another league-winning manager in Matt Beard and set about assembling a squad of full-time professional players, with the result being a place in the SSE Women's

2019 was a truly special occasion honouring one of our all-time greats, while the Upton Gardens development is filled with poignant reminders of the Club's long and illustrious presence in the area.

The Club may have moved to an iconic new home in May 2016, but West Ham remains at the very heart of the community of east London and south Essex.

FA Cup final, which saw the Irons take on Manchester City at Wembley.

**The Academy of Football** continued to thrive, too, with the multi-million pound redevelopment of the Club's historic Chadwell Heath training ground being completed, no fewer than six graduates being selected by Pellegrini and Declan Rice making his full England debut.

The advent of **The Players' Project** — the most ambitious and integrated community programme ever created by a Premier League club — and the continued excellence of the Club's award-winning Foundation mean thousands of local people, from all backgrounds, benefitted from the Hammers' presence.

While the present is full of encouragement and the future looks bright, the Club will never forget the past, with the history and heritage of the past 124 years continuing to be recognised, both at London Stadium and at West Ham's former home at Boleyn Ground.

At London Stadium, the opening of the **Billy Bonds Stand** in March

All in all, the 2018/19 season was one which everyone associated with West Ham United will always be proud of.

# WORDSEARCH

| | | | | | | | | | | | |
|---|---|---|---|---|---|---|---|---|---|---|---|
| N | D | N | A | L | L | O | H | H | M | Y | G |
| E | T | B | R | O | O | K | I | N | G | D | N |
| L | R | B | N | T | K | G | F | T | E | H | K |
| L | L | R | R | P | B | D | H | V | Y | B | J |
| A | B | L | I | U | R | L | O | L | W | S | X |
| N | P | K | A | A | S | N | V | G | D | G | P |
| X | E | A | P | Y | S | H | K | N | C | N | E |
| B | N | M | R | H | L | C | O | X | R | I | A |
| K | A | Z | I | K | N | B | X | P | O | T | R |
| L | T | R | A | W | E | T | S | R | S | R | S |
| L | E | X | Y | N | B | S | D | Y | S | A | O |
| N | N | E | I | G | H | B | O | U | R | M | N |

Can you find the following West Ham United words and phrases in the wordsearch? Answers can be found on page 59

Answers can be found on page 59

| | | |
|---|---|---|
| **ALLEN** | **DEVONSHIRE** | **NEIGHBOUR** |
| **BONDS** | **HOLLAND** | **PARKES** |
| **BROOKING** | **LAMPARD** | **PEARSON** |
| **BRUSH** | **LYALL** | **PIKE** |
| **CROSS** | **MARTIN** | **STEWART** |

WEST HAM
UNITED

# LUKASZ
# FABIANSKI

# MANUEL PELLEGRINI

A tough-tackling defender as a player, Manuel Pellegrini spent his entire career with one club, Universidad de Chile, making more than 500 appearances, earning 28 caps for his country and a degree in civil engineering.

Unsurprisingly, Pellegrini kicked-off his managerial career with the same club in 1988. Since then, however, he has coached 12 different clubs in Chile, Ecuador, Argentina, Spain, England and China!

After winning league titles in Ecuador and Argentina, he crossed the Atlantic Ocean in 2004 to take charge of Spanish club Villarreal. There, he enjoyed huge success, winning the UEFA Intertoto Cup and guiding The Yellow Submarine to the UEFA Champions League semi-finals!

Those achievements saw Pellegrini appointed Real Madrid manager in 2009 and it was during his time at the Estadio Santiago Bernabeu that Real signed Cristiano Ronaldo from Manchester United.

Despite losing just seven of his 48 matches in charge, Pellegrini left Real after a single season before joining Malaga in November 2010, and again guided a previously unfancied team to the Champions League knockout stages.

He was on the move again in 2013, to Manchester City, where he quickly became a popular figure by winning the Premier League title and EFL Cup in his first season at the helm.

Following three seasons in Manchester and 18 months in China with Hebei China Fortune, Pellegrini arrived at London Stadium in June

**Pellegrini has managed Man City and Real Madrid!**

14

**Born:**
16 September 1953, Santiago, Chile

**Clubs played for:**
Universidad de Chile

**International caps/goals:**
28/1

**Clubs managed:**
Universidad de Chile,
Palestino,
O'Higgins,
Universidad Catolica,
Palestino,
LDU Quito,
San Lorenzo,
River Plate,
Villarreal,
Real Madrid,
Malaga,
Manchester City,
Hebei China Fortune,
West Ham United

**Honours won:**
English Premier League (1),
EFL Cup (2),
Copa Chile (1),
Copa Interamericana (1),
Ecuadorian Serie A (1),
Argentinian Primera Division (2),
Copa Mercosur (1),
UEFA Intertoto Cup (1)

2018, becoming the first South American to manage West Ham United and the 17th full-time manager in the Club's history.

15

CROSS OUT ALL THE LETTERS THAT APPEAR MORE THAN ONCE AND UNSCRAMBLE THOSE LEFT TO REVEAL THE NAME OF A PLAYER.

HOW MANY PAIRS OF HAMMERS CAN YOU COUNT?

THE PLAYER IS... ......................................

'GETTING SHIRTY'

FILA

Dr. Martens

WHICH PERIOD DID WE WEAR THIS SHIRT?

A: 1996/97
B: 1999/01
C: 2005/07

WHICH HAMMERS LEGEND IS THIS?

THE PLAYER IS... ..........................................

1

# LUKASZ FABIANSKI

**Born:**
18 April 1985, Kostrzyn nad Odrą, Poland

**Clubs:**
Lech Poznan, Legia Warsaw, Arsenal, Swansea City

**International caps/clean sheets:**
50/21

- Became the first Pole to play for West Ham United when he debuted at Liverpool on 12 August 2018
- Had made more Premier League appearances than any other Pole (219) at the end of the 2018/19 season
- Was voted Hammer of the Year at the end of his debut season, 2018/19, at London Stadium

# JOSEPH ANANG

**Born:**
8 June 2000, Ghana

**Clubs:**
None

- Joined West Ham United after a successful trial period in July 2017, having travelled to England from Ghana to pursue his dream of becoming a professional footballer
- Appeared regularly in Premier League 2 and the Checkatrade Trophy as he battled Nathan Trott for a place in the Hammers' U23 side
- Was part of the first-team squad during pre-season in both 2018/19 and 2019/20, travelling to Switzerland and Austria

# ROBERTO

10 February 1986, Madrid, Spain

Atletico Madrid, Gimnastic (loan), Recreativo, Atletico Madrid, Zaragoza (loan), Benfica, Zaragoza, Atletico Madrid, Olympiacos (loan), Olympiacos, Espanyol, Malaga (loan)

- Came through the ranks at Atletico Madrid, making his La Liga debut at Osasuna at the age of 19 in December 2005, and appeared in the UEFA Champions League for the first time for the same club at FC Porto in September 2009
- Kept 13 clean sheets in 25 Primeira Liga appearances as Benfica won the title in 2010/11
- Won three straight Superleague Greece titles with Olympiacos between 2014-16, keeping 52 clean sheets in 88 matches, and the Greek Cup in 2015

# DAVID MARTIN

**Born:**
22 January 1986, Romford, England

**Clubs:**
Wimbledon, MK Dons, Liverpool, Accrington Stanley (loan), Leicester City (loan), Tranmere Rovers (loan), Leeds United (loan), Derby County (loan), MK Dons, Millwall

- Is the son of former West Ham United defender and captain and England international Alvin Martin, and the older brother of Northampton Town full-back Joe Martin
- Kept ten clean sheets in 25 appearances in helping Leicester City win the EFL League One title in 2008/09, during a loan spell from Liverpool
- Spent seven seasons with Milton Keynes Dons, winning promotion from League One in 2014/15 and Player of the Year honours in 2015/16

# 7 THINGS YOU PROBABLY DIDN'T KNOW ABOUT DECLAN RICE

**1** Declan Rice joined West Ham United at the age of 14 in summer 2013, having previously played schoolboy football for Grey Court School in Richmond-upon-Thames!

**2** Declan Rice became the first teenager to make 50 first-team appearances for West Ham United since fellow deep-lying midfielder Michael Carrick did so in May 2001, reaching the landmark in December 2018.

**3** No West Ham United player made more successful tackles or accurate passes during the 2018/19 Premier League season than Rice, who beat Felipe Anderson into second place in both categories!

**4** Declan Rice names his best friends in football as his former Chelsea Academy teammates Mason Mount and Dan Kemp and current West Ham United teammate Ryan Fredericks.

**5** He won the Young Hammer of the Year three times in a row between 2017-19, becoming the first Academy of Football graduate to win the award on three occasions!

**6** Declan Rice's childhood hero was former Chelsea and England defender John Terry.

**7** When Declan Rice scored his first goal for West Ham United in a 1-0 Premier League victory over Arsenal in January 2019, he became the first Hammer to score a home winner against the Gunners since Marlon Harewood in November 2006, when Rice himself was just seven-years-old!

41

AUTOGRAPH:

DECLAN RICE

# JACK WILSHERE'S Q&A

**What's your guilty pleasure?**
Dirty Burger! It's the best burger in London, maybe in the UK!

**Who was your first club as a kid?**
My first club was a local team called Knebworth.

**What position did you play in as a kid?** On the left wing.

**Who was your hero?** Paolo Di Canio.

**What's your go-to dish if you had one last chance to impress your missus?** I once made a seafood paella. It took me about four hours, but it was lovely!

**Who's your best friend in football?**
Probably Wojciech Szczęszny. I lived with him for a couple of years – don't tell Lukasz Fabianski!

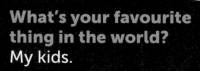

**What's your favourite stadium to play in?** The Camp Nou in Barcelona was good.

**What match was your best ever performance?** Probably for England against Brazil. We won 2-1 at home.

Frank Lampard and Wayne Rooney scored. Ronaldinho played in the game as well. Unreal!

**What's your favourite App on your phone?** Snapchat.

**What's your hidden talent?**
I'm not a bad singer!

**What type of music do you listen to before a game?** I listen to every type of music. Before a game, it's usually Drake.

**Who's the best player you've ever played with?** Robin van Persie.

**And the best player you've played against?** Lionel Messi.

**What's your favourite thing in the world?** My kids.

**Describe yourself in three words.** Handsome, intelligent, and tall!

# WILSHERE'S 'W' XI

The England international midfielder selects a team of players whose surnames begin with the same letter as his!

**GK**

Richard **Wright**

**RB**

Kyle **Walker**

**CB**

Jonathan **Woodgate**

**LB**

Nigel **Winterburn**

**RM**

Theo **Walcott**

**CM**

Ray **Wilkins**

**CM**

Harry **Winks**

**LM**

Willian

**RF**

Paulo **Wanchope**

**CF**

Ian **Wright**

**LF**

Danny **Welbeck**

23

WEST HAM UNITED LONDON

AUTOGRAPH:

MARK NOBLE

## MARK NOBLE

Answer:

## DECLAN RICE

Answer:

# MATCH THE FACT TO THE HAMMER

## JACK WILSHERE

Answer:

## ISSA DIOP

Answer:

## CARLOS SANCHEZ

Answer:

## PABLO FORNALS

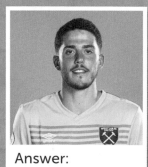

Answer:

## LUKASZ FABIANSKI

Answer:

## SEBASTIEN HALLER

Answer:

## ARTHUR MASUAKU

Answer:

## MANUEL LANZINI

Answer:

1. I have two children — a son Archie and daughter Delilah Grace

2. I have played professional football in Uruguay, France, Spain, Italy and England

3. I have played professional football in Argentina, Brazil, the United Arab Emirates and England

4. I earned my 50th cap for my country in a UEFA Euro 2020 qualifier win over Israel in June 2018

5. I am the most-expensive signing in West Ham United's history

6. I am West Ham United's all-time record Premier League appearance maker

7. I won the UEFA European U21 Championship title in 2018

8. I won two Greek Superleague titles playing alongside Roberto

9. I have won the Young Hammer of the Year award three times

10. I was made captain of French club Toulouse while I was still a teenager

Answers on page 59

# EAT LIKE A HAMMER

West Ham United players keep themselves in shape and fuelled for their next match or training session by following a healthy, balanced and nutritional diet. Here are some tips to do likewise!

## Eat a balanced diet

Next time you are tempted to reach for a chocolate bar or walk into a fast-food restaurant, think again! Instead of relying on convenience foods, you should try consuming a healthy variety of carbohydrates, proteins and vegetables. Start by eating at least five portions of fruit or vegetables every day. Fat is not always a bad thing, either, as fish and low-fat cheeses are among the foods which contain healthy 'good' fats which can provide your body with the fuel it needs.

## Live in a protein world

Your body uses protein to build and repair tissue, including bones, muscles, cartilage, skin, blood, hair and nails, so it's very important to ensure you consume enough of it! When you're feeling peckish, choose

a snack that's high in protein, rather than an alternative that is high in fat. Things like protein mousses and shakes, sports bars and flapjacks are perfect. You can obviously buy these from a shop, but making them from scratch at home is much more fun!

## Reach for the superfoods

'Superfoods' are those that contain higher-than-average levels of essential nutrients and include things like avocados, blueberries, beetroot and quinoa.

All of these are great providers of vitamins and minerals that the body needs for a variety of reasons, from digestion to fuelling up to post-exercise recovery.

# Eggs and cereal

With school, college, university or a job to do, many amateur footballers simply do not have the time to prepare the meals that professional players enjoy having made for them on a daily basis.

For that reason, it is important to have food available that is quick and easy to get ready and eat. Two foods which fit the bill are eggs and cereals, which provide you with a ready source of energy-boosting calories. Omelettes are simple to make, as are scrambled eggs, while you could also rustle up a bowl of sugar-free cereal like granola, with some plain yoghurt, both of which are great meals to have when you get home from a sapping training session or match.

# Go fish!

Ask any West Ham United player, male or female, of any age, and they will tell you that fish is a huge part of their diet. Not only is it rich in protein, which we have already explained the benefits of, but fish is packed with the healthy oils and fats the body uses for energy and recovery.

Sushi is very easy to eat, light, and packed with goodness, but it will not make you feel bloated before you train or play, either.
While all fish delivers the healthy fats your body needs, non-white fish like salmon or trout are among the richest in omega-3 fatty acids, which have a wide range of benefits for your physical and mental health.

# Everything in moderation!

While these tips are great for living a healthy lifestyle, as an amateur sportsperson, you need to remember that moderation and balance are important, too.

Don't deprive yourself of every treat, but just enjoy those 'naughty', less-healthy foods and drinks less often than you did before.

Generally speaking, if you are maintaining a steady bodyweight, feel energetic and positive, you are probably eating and drinking the right things!

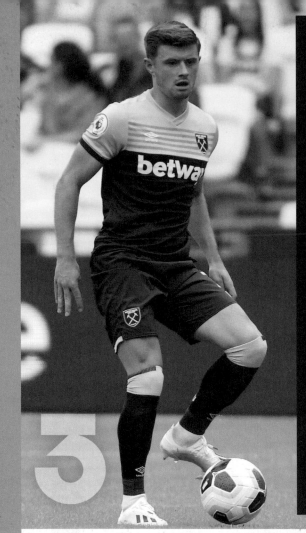

# DEFENDERS

## AARON CRESSWELL

**Born:**
15 December 1989, Liverpool, England

**Clubs:**
Tranmere Rovers, Ipswich Town

**International caps/goals:** 3/0

- Joined Tranmere Rovers after representing Liverpool as a schoolboy before spending three seasons in the Championship with Ipswich Town between 2011-14
- Won the Hammer of the Year and Players' Player of the Year awards at the end of his debut season with West Ham United in 2014/15
- Made his senior England debut in a friendly international with Spain at Wembley Stadium in November 2016

## PABLO ZABALETA

**Born:**
16 January 1985, Buenos Aires, Argentina

**Clubs:**
San Lorenzo, Espanyol, Manchester City

**International caps/goals:** 58/0

- Won Gold at the 2008 Olympics in China before starting Argentina's 2014 FIFA World Cup final defeat by Germany in Brazil
- Enjoyed nine successful seasons with Manchester City between 2008-17, winning two Premier League titles, two EFL Cups and one FA Cup and being named in the 2012/13 PFA Premier League Team of the Year
- Joined West Ham United in summer 2017 and missed just one Premier League match in his first season in east London

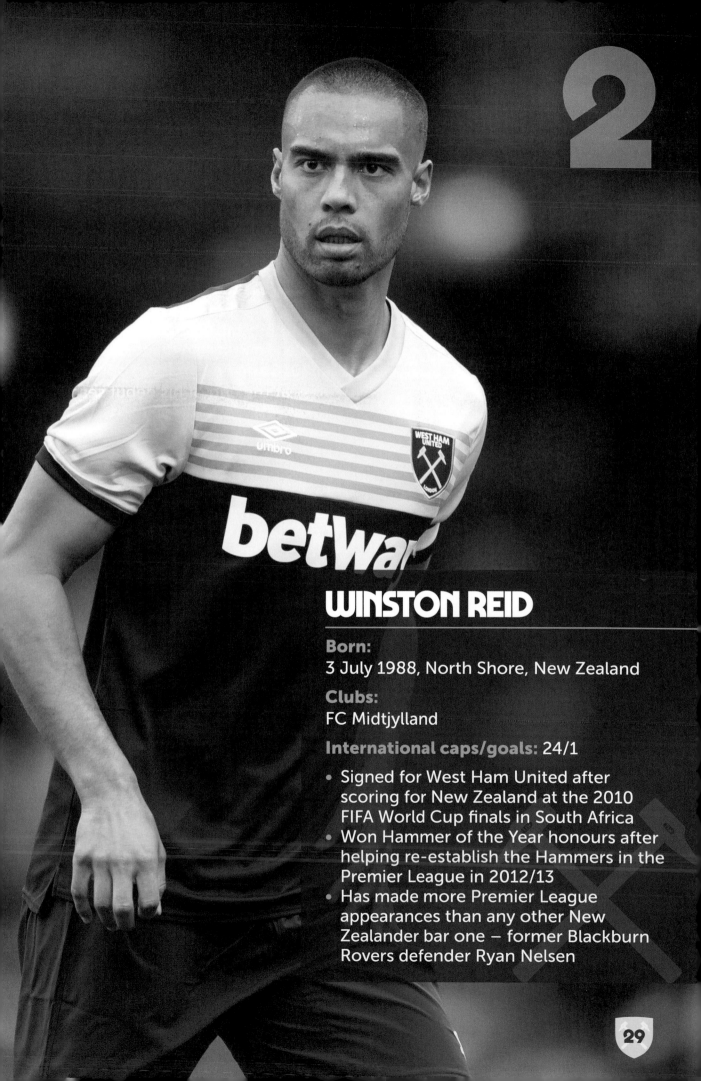

# WINSTON REID

**Born:**
3 July 1988, North Shore, New Zealand

**Clubs:**
FC Midtjylland

**International caps/goals:** 24/1

- Signed for West Ham United after scoring for New Zealand at the 2010 FIFA World Cup finals in South Africa
- Won Hammer of the Year honours after helping re-establish the Hammers in the Premier League in 2012/13
- Has made more Premier League appearances than any other New Zealander bar one – former Blackburn Rovers defender Ryan Nelsen

4

## FABIAN BALBUENA

**Born:**
23 August 1991, Ciudad del Este, Paraguay

**Clubs:**
Cerro Porteno, Rubio Nu, Nacional, Libertad, Corinthians

**International caps/goals:** 11/0

- Played in his home country until the age of 24, winning the Division Intermedia title with Cerro Porteno in 2011 and Primera Division closing championship with Libertad in 2014
- Moved to Brazilian giants Corinthians in 2016 and enjoyed two outstanding seasons in Sao Paulo, winning Serie A, two state championships and the Campeonato Brasileiro Golden Ball award
- Joined West Ham United in July 2018, making his debut at Liverpool the following month and scoring his first goal for the Club at Leicester City in October last year

23

## ISSA DIOP

**Born:**
9 January 1997, Toulouse, France

**Clubs:**
Toulouse

- Joined West Ham United from Ligue 1 club Toulouse on a five-year contract for a then Club-record fee in June 2018
- Was a first-team regular at Toulouse after breaking into the Ligue 1 side at the age of 18 in November 2015, making 85 appearances for his hometown club
- Capped at every age-group level from U16 to U21, winning the UEFA European U19 Championship with France in 2016 and scoring in a 4-0 victory over Italy in the final

**20**

# GONCALO CARDOSO

**Born:**
21 October 2000, Marco de Canaveses, Portugal

**Clubs:**
AD Marco 09, Penafiel, Boavista

- Began his professional career with Porto-based Portuguese club Boavista, making his debut two weeks short of his 18th birthday in a Primeira Division victory over Desportivo Aves in October 2018
- The tall, ball-playing defender was part of the Portugal side which finished runners-up at the 2019 UEFA European U19 Championship finals, scoring in his country's group-stage win over Italy
- Joined West Ham United on a long-term contract in August 2019, becoming the fifth of the Irons' six senior summer signings

**24**

# RYAN FREDERICKS

**Born:**
10 October 1992, London, England

**Clubs:**
Tottenham Hotspur, Brentford (loan), Millwall (loan), Middlesbrough (loan), Bristol City, Fulham

- Joined West Ham United in July 2018 on a four-year contract, becoming Manuel Pellegrini's first signing as Hammers boss
- Arrived at London Stadium on the back of a memorable 2017/18 campaign with Fulham, having won promotion to the Premier League and been named in the PFA Championship Team of the Year
- A full-back blessed with blistering pace, Fredericks made his Tottenham Hotspur debut alongside Harry Kane in August 2011

## ARTHUR MASUAKU

**Born:**
7 November 1993, Lille, France

**Clubs:**
Valenciennes, Olympiacos

**International caps/goals:** 4/1

- Exciting left-sided defender or midfielder who arrived at West Ham United after two successful seasons with Greek giants Olympiacos in summer 2016
- A France-born defender who began his professional career with Valenciennes before winning back-to-back Superleague Greece titles
- Capped by DR Congo at senior international level, appearing for the country of his parents' birth at the 2019 Africa Cup of Nations finals

## BEN JOHNSON

**Born:**
24 January 2000, London, England

**Clubs:**
None

- Academy of Football graduate who joined West Ham United at the age of seven in 2007 and was converted from right winger to full-back as a teenager
- Made his first-team debut at left-back at Premier League champions Manchester City in February 2019
- Is a cousin of former England defenders Paul Parker and Ledley King

# ANGELO OGBONNA

**Born:**
23 May 1988, Cassino, Italy

**Clubs:**
Torino, Crotone (loan), Juventus

**International caps/goals:** 13/0

- Signed for West Ham United from Italian champions Juventus in summer 2015, having won back-to-back Serie A titles in Turin
- An Italy international central defender, who can also play at left-back, he started his career with Torino before moving across the city in 2013
- Etched his name into Hammers folklore with his unforgettable extra-time FA Cup winner against Liverpool at the Boleyn Ground in February 2016 – the Irons' final FA Cup victory at their former home

# STARS OF THE FUTURE?

West Ham United have been associated with the production of outstanding young players for more than 60 years.

The Academy of Football has provided the Hammers with dozens of first-team players since its formation in the 1950s, including future England captains, FA Cup, European Cup Winners' Cup and Hammer of the Year award winners.

During the 2018/19 season, no fewer than six Academy graduates featured at senior level in Claret and Blue, with more set to follow in their footsteps during the current campaign.

Here, we profile the players who hope to follow the likes of Bobby Moore, Rio Ferdinand and Mark Noble and become West Ham's stars of the future...

## NATHAN TROTT

**Position:** Goalkeeper
**Born:** 21 November 1998, Paget, Bermuda
⊙: @nathan.trott

Bermuda-born goalkeeper Nathan Trott joined West Ham United following a successful trial period in January 2016, having initially been recommended to the Club by former Hammer and fellow countryman Clyde Best.

A schoolboy midfielder, Trott is not only an agile shot-stopper, but also possesses superb distribution skills and technique.

The young goalkeeper switched international allegiance to England in early 2017 and was part of the Young Lions squad that won the UEFA European U19 Championship in June of the same year.

# KRISZTIAN HEGYI

**Position:** Goalkeeper
**Born:** 24 September 2002, Budapest, Hungary

Hungarian stopper Krisztian Hegyi joined the Hammers from Haladas in his homeland in the summer of 2019.

Personally scouted by first-team goalkeeper coach Xavi Valero, the highly-rated stopper represented Hungary at the 2019 UEFA U17 European Championship finals and at the 2019 FIFA U19 World Cup in Brazil.

The teenager was part of West Ham United's pre-season touring party in Switzerland in July.

# BEN JOHNSON

**Position:** Full-back
**Born:** 24 January 2000, Waltham Forest, England

Ben Johnson has thrived since being converted from a winger into an attack-minded right-back as a schoolboy.

Johnson has been with West Ham United since the age of seven and appeared regularly in every age-group side he has featured in, impressing with his maturity, athleticism and work ethic.

The defender, who counts former England internationals Paul Parker and Ledley King among his close relatives, made his first-team debut at Manchester City in February 2019 and was rewarded with a new long-term contract the following month.

# JEREMY NGAKIA

**Position:** Full-back
**Born:** 7 September 2000, London, England
⊙: @jeremy_ngakia

An attacking full-back capable of playing on either side of the back four, Jeremy Ngakia is a strong and speedy player who is always on the front foot.

After breaking into the U18s while still a schoolboy, Ngakia became a full-time scholar in 2018 and quickly progressed to U23 football, making his Premier League 2 debut against Tottenham Hotspur at the age of 17 in February 2018.

# AJIBOLA ALESE

**Position:** Centre-back
**Born:** 17 January 2001, London, England
:camera: : @jeremy_ngakia

Centre-back Ajibola Alese continued his impressive ascent through the Academy of Football ranks by signing his first professional contract with West Ham United in the summer of 2018.

A year later, the defender won the Dylan Tombides Award for being the Academy's outstanding performer during the 2018/19 season.

A strong all-round player, Alese has been capped by England at age-group level, appearing at the 2018 UEFA European U17 Championship finals.

# CONOR COVENTRY

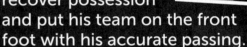

**Position:** Midfielder
**Born:** 25 March 2000, Waltham Forest, England
:camera: : @conorcoventry1

Conor Coventry is a deep-lying midfielder who won West Ham United's Dylan Tombides Award at the end of the 2017/18 season and has regularly captained the U23s.

A Republic of Ireland U21 international, Coventry has an all-round game which enables him to both recover possession and put his team on the front foot with his accurate passing.

The teenager made his senior Hammers debut in the 8-0 EFL Cup third-round win over Macclesfield Town at London Stadium in September 2018.

# JOE POWELL

**Position:** Midfielder
**Born:** 30 October 1998, London, England
:bird: : @JoePowell_10

Joe Powell is a versatile performer able to fill a variety of roles across the midfield and at left-back.

A creative left-sided player, Powell has played regularly for West Ham United's age-group sides since joining the Club as a schoolboy, captaining the U18s and U23s to boot.

Powell registered two assists for Grady Diangana on his memorable first-team debut in the 8-0 Carabao Cup third-round win over Macclesfield Town at London Stadium on 26 September 2018. He signed a new one-year contract in May.

# DAN KEMP

**Position:** Midfielder
**Born:** 11 January 1999, Sidcup, England
📷 : @dankemp11

A diminutive attacking midfielder or winger, Dan Kemp moved to West Ham United from Chelsea in November 2015.

The Kent-born player celebrated signing a new three-year contract in June 2018 by scoring a career-high six Premier League 2 goals last season.

Capped by England at U19 and U20 levels, Kemp was earlier part of the Hammers squad which lifted the Premier League Cup in May 2016.

# GRADY DIANGANA

**Position:** Winger
**Born:** 19 April 1998, Kinshasa, DR Congo

An exciting player who joined West Ham United at the age of 12, Grady Diangana can play in a variety of positions across the forward line.

The right-sided attacker was an influential member of the U23 side which won promotion to Premier League 2 Division 1 in 2016/17 before forcing his way into the first-team picture last season.

After scoring twice on his debut in an 8-0 Carabao Cup victory against Macclesfield Town, the England U20 international went on to make 21 senior appearances for Manuel Pellegrini in 2018/19.

# NATHAN HOLLAND

**Position:** Winger
**Born:** 19 June 1998, Wythenshawe, England
◎: @nho11and

Winger Nathan Holland joined West Ham United from Everton in January 2017.

The Manchester-born attacker had already been capped by England at U16, U17, U18 and U19 levels prior to joining the Hammers, and has continued his development since moving to east London.

Holland's ability saw him rewarded with a senior debut in the EFL Cup third-round win over Bolton Wanderers at London Stadium in September 2017. He was also named on the first-team bench at Manchester United in April 2019.

# AMADOU DIALLO

**Position:** Winger
**Born:** 15 February 2003, Conakry, Guinea

Skilful and speedy, Amadou Diallo is a West Ham United player of immense promise. So highly rated is England U16 international Diallo within the Academy of Football that he was just 14 years and six months old when he debuted in the U18 Premier League at Arsenal in August 2017.

The forward featured seven times for the U18s while still an U15 by age-group, starting three times. As an U16 schoolboy, he netted his first goals at U18 level in a 3-2 Premier League Cup victory over Manchester City in November 2018, before becoming a full-time scholar last summer.

AUTOGRAPH:

SÉBASTIEN HALLER

# COLOURING TIME

Show off your artistic skills by colouring in this photo of West Ham United mascot Hammerhead on the opposite page.
Be careful to stay inside the lines!

FIND EIGHT DIFFERENCES BETWEEN THESE TWO IMAGES OF MICHAIL ANTONIO CELEBRATING HIS GOAL VS LEICESTER CITY LAST SEASON?

CAN YOU NAME THE FOUR PREMIER LEAGUE CLUBS THAT MAKE UP THIS CREST?

A. _ _ _ _ _ _ _ _

B. _ _ _ _ _ _ _ _ _ _ /
_ _ _ _ _ _ _ _

C. _ _ _ _ _ _ _ /
_ _ _

D. _ _ _ _ _ _ _ /
_ _ _ _

## MANUEL LANZINI

**Born:**
15 February 1993, Ituzaingó, Argentina

**Clubs:**
River Plate, Fluminense (loan), Al Jazira Club

**International caps/goals:** 4/1

- Exciting Argentina international attacking midfielder who has got West Ham United fans off their seats regularly since joining the Club in summer 2015
- Nicknamed 'La Joya', Spanish for 'The Jewel', the playmaker won a league title with River Plate in his home city of Buenos Aires
- Made his senior debut for Argentina against Brazil in June 2017 in the Australian city of Melbourne

## ROBERT SNODGRASS

**Born:**
7 September 1987, Glasgow, Scotland

**Clubs:**
Livingston, Stirling Albion (loan), Leeds United, Norwich City, Hull City, Aston Villa (loan)

**International caps/goals:** 26/7

- Left-footed creative midfielder who has made his name by delivering dangerous balls into the box and scoring spectacular goals of his own
- Began his career with local club Livingston before moving south and representing English clubs Leeds United, Norwich City, Hull City, Aston Villa and West Ham United
- Scored an international hat-trick for Scotland in a 2018 FIFA World Cup qualifying win in Malta in September 2016

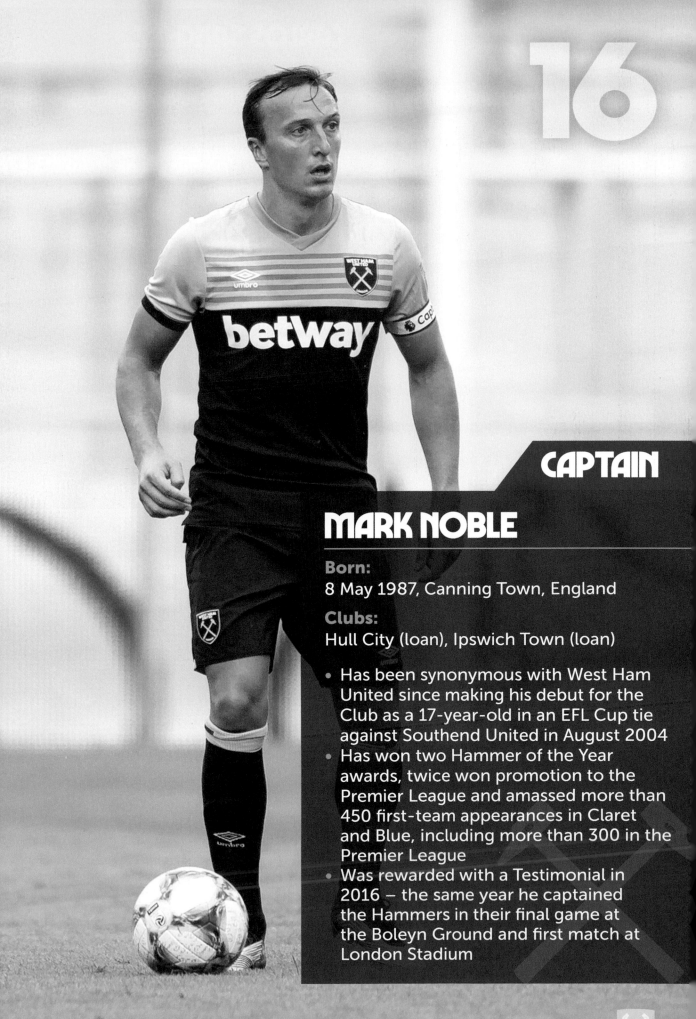

## CAPTAIN

# MARK NOBLE

**Born:**
8 May 1987, Canning Town, England

**Clubs:**
Hull City (loan), Ipswich Town (loan)

- Has been synonymous with West Ham United since making his debut for the Club as a 17-year-old in an EFL Cup tie against Southend United in August 2004
- Has won two Hammer of the Year awards, twice won promotion to the Premier League and amassed more than 450 first-team appearances in Claret and Blue, including more than 300 in the Premier League
- Was rewarded with a Testimonial in 2016 – the same year he captained the Hammers in their final game at the Boleyn Ground and first match at London Stadium

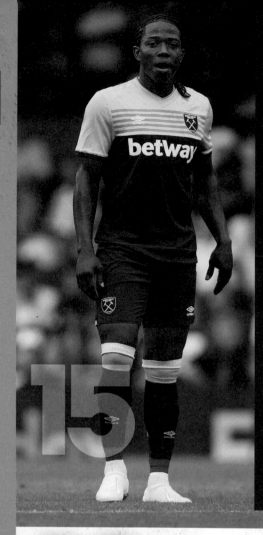

**15**

# CARLOS SANCHEZ

**Born:**
6 February 1986, Quibdo, Colombia

**Clubs:**
River Plate Montevideo, Valenciennes, Elche, Aston Villa, Fiorentina (loan), Fiorentina, Espanyol (loan)

**International caps/goals:** 82/0

- Defensive midfielder who joined West Ham United from Italian club Fiorentina in August 2018, returning to England after a previous spell with Aston Villa
- Played professionally in Uruguay, France and Spain, spending six seasons in Ligue 1 with Valenciennes between 2007-13
- Debuted for Colombia in 2007 and has since appeared for his country at three Copa America tournaments and the 2014 and 2018 FIFA World Cup finals

**19**

# JACK WILSHERE

**Born:**
1 January 1992, Stevenage, England

**Clubs:**
Arsenal, Bolton Wanderers (loan), AFC Bournemouth (loan)

**International caps/goals:** 34/2

- Joined West Ham United on a three-year contract in July 2018, ending a 17-year association with Arsenal
- Won two FA Cups and the FA Youth Cup with the Gunners, making nearly 200 senior appearances and being voted PFA Young Player of the Year in 2010/11
- Capped more than 30 times, Wilshere was part of the England squads at the 2014 FIFA World Cup and UEFA Euro 2016 finals

**41**

# DECLAN RICE

**Born:**
14 January 1999, Kingston upon Thames, England

**Clubs:**
Chelsea

**International caps/goals:** 3/0

- Deep-lying midfielder or centre-back who joined West Ham United's Academy of Football at the age of 14 following his release by boyhood club Chelsea
- Captained the Hammers at U16, U18 and U23 levels before making his first-team debut in a Premier League win at Burnley in the final game of the 2016/17 season
- Two-time Hammer of the Year runner-up who was given his senior England debut in a UEFA Euro 2020 win over Czech Republic at Wembley Stadium in March 2019

# PABLO FORNALS

**Born:**
22 February 1996, Castellon, Spain

**Clubs:**
Malaga, Villarreal

**International caps/goals:** 2/0

- Joined West Ham United from Spanish club Villarreal in June 2019, having impressed for both the Yellow Submarine and Malaga over four seasons in La Liga
- Was part of the Spain team which won the UEFA European U21 Championship in June 2019, scoring two goals and assisting a third
- Made his senior debut for Spain in a friendly win over Bosnia and Herzegovina in May 2016, aged just 20

**18**

# TRAIN LIKE A HAMMER

## Speed and Agility

Being able to move and change direction quickly are vital to wrong-footing your opponent. Here are some exercises to speed up your feet!

# Shuttle runs

They might be old-fashioned, but shuttle runs are still a great way to increase agility and speed. Place two cones 20 to 30 yards apart, and a third midway between the two, but five yards to the left. Start at the middle cone, then sprint to one of the ends, along the long edge of the triangle to the other end, then back to the middle. Repeat this four more times. To add some variety, replace sprints with giant strides, heel flicks, high knees or by skipping!

# Tiptoes

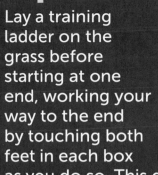

Lay a training ladder on the grass before starting at one end, working your way to the end by touching both feet in each box as you do so. This drill improves balance, speed and agility, while also increasing muscle strength.

# Agility sprints

Set up a square of four cones with ten yards between the corners and number them 1-4. Have someone call out the numbers randomly and sprint between them at high speed for 30-second intervals.

# Weave in and out

Set up training poles or cones at three-yard intervals in a straight line. Then set up a second line of poles or cones in a parallel line three yards to the left, halfway between the first line, creating a slalom course. Start at one end and sprint to the other then back again, weaving in and out, with an emphasis on quick side-steps.

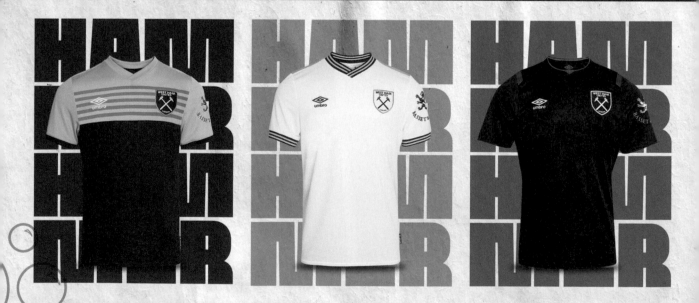

AUTOGRAPH:

WEST HAM
UNITED

18

PABLO
FORNALS

# 8 REASONS TO LOVE THE LONDON STADIUM

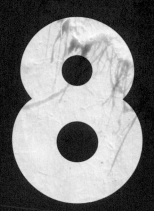

1975 FA Cup Winners

**1** Built between 2008-11, London Stadium was originally constructed on former industrial land in Stratford, surrounded by canals and rivers, for the 2012 Summer Olympic and Paralympic Games. The event, which had the motto 'Inspire a Generation', saw more than 15,000 athletes from 204 nations compete in 28 different sports. Team GB won 185 medals across the two events.

**3** West Ham United officially began life at London Stadium in August 2016, when Italian Serie A champions Juventus were the visitors. A thrilling match was won 3-2 by the visitors, with Andy Carroll scoring both goals for the Hammers.

**2** Following the 2012 Games, London Stadium was subject to bids from potential future users, with West Ham United being named as the preferred bidders in December 2012 and granted a 99-year lease in March 2013.

**4** London Stadium is now a multi-use venue open all-year-round. Since the 2012 Games, it has played host to the World Athletics and Para Athletics Championships, Race of Champions, Rugby World Cup, international rugby league, Major League Baseball and concerts given by artists including the Rolling Stones, Robbie Williams, Beyonce and Jay-Z, Foo Fighters and Muse.

**5** Situated on the purpose-built Queen Elizabeth Olympic Park, London Stadium is the best-connected football ground in the country, being served by National Rail, London Overground, London Underground, Docklands Light Railway, London Bus and National Express coach services!

**6** London Stadium currently has a capacity of 60,000 spectators for football matches, meaning West Ham United's home is the fourth-largest club ground in England behind Manchester United's Old Trafford, Tottenham Hotspur Stadium and Arsenal's Emirates Stadium. The Hammers are looking at the possibility of increasing the capacity to 62,500, which would make it larger than both Tottenham and Arsenal's home stadia.

**7** London Stadium is open throughout the year for Stadium Tours, which enable visitors to go behind-the-scenes to pitchside, the West Ham United dressing room, Club London hospitality areas and also visit the Stadium Store. Some tours are even led by Hammers legends!

**8** Three of London Stadium's four stands are named in honour of West Ham United all-time greats. The Bobby Moore and Sir Trevor Brooking Stands were opened in August 2016, before the East Stand was renamed the Billy Bonds Stand in tribute to the Hammers' two-time FA Cup-winning captain and all-time appearance record-holder in April 2019.

7

## ANDRIY YARMOLENKO

**Born:**
23 October 1989, Leningrad, Soviet Union

**Clubs:**
Desna Chernihiv, Dynamo Kyiv, Borussia Dortmund

**International caps/goals: 80/36**

- Exciting, prolific and versatile forward who joined West Ham United from Borussia Dortmund in July 2018.
- Enjoyed a hugely successful career with Dynamo Kyiv and the Ukrainian national team, scoring more than 175 goals and registering well over 100 assists
- Four-time Ukrainian Footballer of the Year who featured for his country at UEFA Euro 2012 and 2016

8

## FELIPE ANDERSON

**Born:**
15 April 1993, Santa Maria, Brazil

**Clubs:**
Santos, Lazio

**International caps/goals: 2/0**

- Joined West Ham United for a Club-record fee in July 2018, having completed five successful seasons in Italy with Lazio
- Came through the ranks at the famous Brazilian club Santos, which also produced superstars Pele, Coutinho, Clodoaldo and Neymar
- Made his senior debut for Brazil against Mexico in June 2015 before winning an Olympic Gold medal in Rio the following year

**30**

# MICHAIL ANTONIO

**Born:**
28 March 1990, Wandsworth, England

**Clubs:**
Tooting & Mitcham United, Reading, Tooting & Mitcham United (loan), Cheltenham Town (loan), Southampton (loan), Colchester United (loan), Sheffield Wednesday (loan), Sheffield Wednesday, Nottingham Forest

- Has emerged as a Premier League star since joining from Championship club Nottingham Forest in September 2015, earning a call-up to the senior England squad
- Starred in the Farewell Boleyn season, scoring in the 3-2 victory over Manchester United in the final game at the Boleyn Ground in May 2016
- A winger with power, pace and an eye for goal, the Londoner was voted Hammer of the Year by supporters at the end of the 2016/17 season

# SEBASTIEN HALLER

**22**

**Born:**
22 June 1994, Ris Orangis, France

**Clubs:**
Auxerre, FC Utrecht (loan), FC Utrecht, Eintracht Frankfurt

- Began his career at French club Auxerre, which also produced future France internationals Eric Cantona, Laurent Blanc, Basile Boli and Djibril Cisse
- Has been capped at every age-group level by France from U17 up to U21, making 20 appearances and scoring 13 goals at the latter
- Scored at a prolific rate for Dutch club Utrecht before moving to Eintracht Frankfurt, where he won the German Cup in Spring 2018

**32**

## XANDE SILVA

**Born:**
16 March 1997, Porto, Portugal

**Clubs:**
Vitoria Guimaraes

- Versatile Portuguese forward who joined West Ham United from Vitoria Guimaraes in August 2018
- Made his senior debut for Vitoria Guimaraes as a 17-year-old in August 2014 and went on to make more than 80 appearances for the club across four seasons
- Capped by Portugal at every age-group level from U15 to U20, appearing at the UEFA European U17 and U19 Championship finals

**27**

## ALBIAN AJETI

**Born:**
26 February 1997, Basel, Switzerland

**Clubs:**
Basel, FC Augsburg, St Gallen (loan), St Gallen, Basel

**International caps/goals:** 3/1

- Born in the Swiss city of Basel, beginning his career with the city's eponymous club at the age of eight
- Scored his first international goal in a UEFA Nations League win over Iceland in September 2018
- Joined West Ham United in August 2019 after scoring at a prolific rate for St Gallen and Basel in the Swiss Super League

# Annual Teaser Answers!

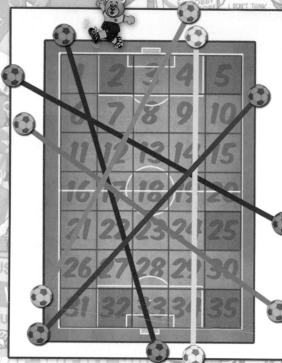

**Unscramble the Player:**
(Pablo) Fornals

**There are 15 pairs of Hammers.**

**Getting Shirty:**
We wore this away shirt
from (B) 1999/01.

**The Hammers Legend is**
Tony Cottee (Toe-Knee Cot-Tea)

The four Premier League clubs
that make up the crest are...
A. Chelsea
B. Sheffield United
C: Manchester City
D: Leicester City

**Bubbles collects four footballs on
the way to his tent.**

**Spot the Difference
Solution:**

WHAT A
BEAUTIFUL CARPET!

58

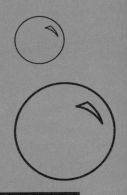

# WORDSEARCH & MATCH THE FACT
## ANSWERS!

```
N  D N A L L O H  H M Y  G
E  T  B R O O K I N G  D  N
L  R  B N T K G F T E H K
L  L R R P B D H V Y B J
A  B L I U R L O L W S X
N  P K A A S N V G D G P
X  E A P Y S H K N C N E
B  N M R H L C O X R I A
K  A Z I K N B X P O T R
L  T R A W E T S R S R S
L  E X Y N B S D Y S A O
N  N E I G H B O U R M N
```

1. WILSHERE
2. SANCHEZ
3. LANZINI
4. FABIANSKI
5. HALLER
6. NOBLE
7. FORNALS
8. MASUAKU
9. RICE
10. DIOP

# WEMBLEY HEROES

**West Ham United upset the odds, and Arsenal, to lift the FA Cup for a third time in May 1980.**

It is 40 years since West Ham United became the last team from outside the top flight to win football's most-famous final.

The Hammers were considered long odds to defeat First Division Arsenal, the reigning FA Cup holders, making their record third successive final appearance, at Wembley Stadium.

However, a football match is played on the pitch and, with sunny skies overhead, John Lyall's Irons shone brighter than Terry Neill's Gunners.

This may not have been the greatest spectacle but no-one from east London was complaining as the eleven men all in white triumphed under the Twin Towers.

West Ham's winner came from the unlikely source of Trevor Brooking's forehead with just 13 minutes on the clock.

In this, the 99th FA Cup final, Alan Devonshire made a trademark run down the left wing before lifting a cross into the penalty area.

Arsenal goalkeeper Pat Jennings could only help the ball on to David Cross, whose shot was blocked. The ball dropped to Stuart Pearson, who mishit his shot across goal, where Brooking reacted quickest, falling back to expertly guide a header past Jennings from eight yards.

It was poetic justice for the elegant Brooking, who had been taunted before the game by the legendary Nottingham Forest manager Brian Clough, who claimed that West Ham's gifted No10 'floats like a butterfly — and stings like one!'

# WEST HAM UNITED 1

Brooking 13

# ARSENAL 0

FA Cup final, Saturday 10 May 1980,
Wembley Stadium
Attendance: 100,000
Referee: George Courtney

As Hammers headed back to the East End for an FA Cup knees-up for the second time in six seasons, Arsenal's agony was compounded by a European Cup Winners' Cup final defeat by Spanish side Valencia just four days later.

With a goal in the bag, Hammers fought like lions, rather than butterflies, while manager Lyall's tactical masterstroke in playing Cross as a lone striker, with Pearson in a withdrawn midfield role, simply left the Gunners unable to find a way past Jennings' opposite number Phil Parkes.

And but for Willie Young's cynical, late trip on the breaking Paul Allen — at 17 years, 256 days the youngest player ever to appear in an FA Cup final — West Ham would surely have extended their final winning margin.

## LINE-UPS

**West Ham United:** Parkes, Stewart, Lampard, Bonds, Martin, Devonshire, Allen, Pearson, Cross, Brooking, Pike
Sub not used: Brush

**Arsenal:** Jennings, Rice, Devine (Nelson), Talbot, O'Leary, Young, Brady, Sunderland, Stapleton, Price, Rix